SLOW COOKER Recipe Book
UK

with COLOURED PHOTOS

Affordable and Easy Meals
to Prepare at Home for your Family
and Friends

CHARLOTTE ELLIS

Copyright 2022 by Charlotte Ellis - All rights reserved.

The following Book is reproduced below with the goal of providing information that is as accurate and reliable as possible. Regardless, purchasing this Book can be seen as consent to the fact that both the publisher and the author of this book are in no way experts on the topics discussed within and that any recommendations or suggestions that are made herein are for entertainment purposes only. Professionals should be consulted as needed prior to undertaking any of the action endorsed herein.

This declaration is deemed fair and valid by both the American Bar Association and the Committee of Publishers Association and is legally binding throughout the United States.

Furthermore, the transmission, duplication, or reproduction of any of the following work including specific information will be considered an illegal act irrespective of if it is done electronically or in print. This extends to creating a secondary or tertiary copy of the work or a recorded copy and is only allowed with the express written consent from the Publisher. All additional right reserved.

The information in the following pages is broadly considered a truthful and accurate account of facts and as such, any inattention, use, or misuse of the information in question by the reader will render any resulting actions solely under their purview. There are no scenarios in which the publisher or the original author of this work can be in any fashion deemed liable for any hardship or damages that may befall them after undertaking information described herein.

Additionally, the information in the following pages is intended only for informational purposes and should thus be thought of as universal. As befitting its nature, it is presented without assurance regarding its prolonged validity or interim quality. Trademarks that are mentioned are done without written consent and can in no way be considered an endorsement from the trademark holder.

TABLE OF CONTENTS

INTRODUCTION 5

    What Is Slow Cooking? 5

    Some tips to use the slow cooker 7

    Caring for Your Slow Cooker 9

    Why Use a Slow Cooker 10

Chapter 1: BREAKFAST RECIPES 12

Chapter 2: READ MEAT RECIPES 19

Chapter 3: POULTRY RECIPES 36

Chapter 4: VEGETARIAN RECIPES 45

Chapter 5: MAIN DISH RECIPES 56

Chapter 6: DESSERTS 68

RECIPES INDEX 79

INTRODUCTION

What Is Slow Cooking?

Slow cookers prepare meals at a low temperature for 4 to 8 hours. The nutrients in the meal remain in the food because of the lower temperature. Any nutrients lost in the liquid due to heat are simply reabsorbed into the food being in a sealed unit, whether using an electric slow cooker or a casserole dish in the oven. Cooking for longer periods enhances flavour and eliminates the need for additional seasoning or sauces. On the other hand, spices and herbs provide richness by imparting their goodness and aroma to the food.

Slow cookers are particularly advantageous for individuals who do not have enough time to prepare lunch. You may put all of the ingredients in the cooker first thing in the morning and program it to produce the perfect dinner for you until lunchtime. Long cooking times allow the food to absorb the majority of the ingredients and infuse the meal with scent.

Yes, the slow cooker (also called a crockpot) can be your magic genie or the shoemaker's elves, doing the work for you while you sleep or while you have other things to do. You throw in all your ingredients, leave it and come back for a ready-to-eat meal. You save time, energy and money but still turn out healthy and delicious food.

Slow cookers are for the seasoned chef as well as the cooking novice because of their versatility. With the slow cooker, you have time to do other stuff. The slow cooker is also safe to leave cooking all day in your home. You can prepare soups to warm you in winter. In summer, while using a well-insulated pot, you can prepare tasty dishes without adding more heat to your home.

You have to admit that slow-cooked food has a distinct flavour that no other cuisine can match. Traditional slow cooking had a number of drawbacks, including the need for regular supervision, which was one of the primary reasons most people abandoned slow cooking. Slow cooking has never been easier than it is now, thanks to the introduction of electric slow cookers. All you have to do now to cook in an electric slow cooker is set the time and temperature, then leave the food in the cooker, covered, and the machine will do the rest. The cooking temperature is kept low by the digitally regulated heating system, which protects the food from burning.

If you have never used a slow cooker before, here's how to use it to make delectable and flavourful meals. First, position the unit on a firm surface close to the power supply. Make sure it's fully clean from the inside out before connecting it in. If not, use a soft dry towel to wipe it away. Remove the pot from the oven and rinse it in cold water. Before returning the cooking pot to the base unit, clean it thoroughly. Before putting everything back together, make sure the base is totally dry from the outside.

If the recipe calls for preheating the liquid, pour it into the slow cooker and cover it. The control panel can be used to set the time and mode. Allow time for it to heat up. To prepare the dinner, combine all ingredients in the slow cooker and keep the liquid level below the maximum fill line, as overfilling can result in leaking. Avoid adding the food because it will make a lot of froth while cooking.

Cover the slow cooker lid and secure it in the grooves of the base unit after adding the food. Set and seal the lid properly to help keep the pressure inside the pot constant. The vapours are trapped by the lid and returned to the food. As a result, the meal takes a bath in its vapours. It's time to start cooking now that everything is in its proper location. Select a temperature mode from the control panel: 1. High, 2. Medium, or 3. Low. After adjusting the mode, you may choose the time and use the adjustment key to increase or reduce the number of minutes. The pot will heat up in a few seconds and steadily cook the meal. It's time for you to unwind and wait for the slow cooker to finish its work.

After the completion beep, the pot will automatically switch to "Keep Warm" mode. This setting keeps your meal warm until you check the gadget and turn it off. Remove the pot's lid and turn off the "Keep Warm" option. Give the cooked food a couple of gentle stirs. Then serve it up. Remember to clean the cooking pot after each cooking session. Because the inside pot is washable, it can be readily cleaned underwater. On the other hand, the metallic housing should only be wiped with a soft cloth. After each session, it's also a good idea to wash the lid.

SOME TIPS TO USE THE SLOW COOKER

Whether you're a working professional, a stay-at-home parent, a student, or a retiree, weeknight dinners just seem to be a challenge to get on the table, don't they? We're all busy rushing around at work or home getting errands done, homework accomplished, household duties looked after, and keeping appointments. And the hour that we should be preparing dinner—from 5 to 6 p.m.—seems to be the busiest!

Some moms of young toddlers call it the witching hour because their young children seem to turn into crazy monsters then. That's why I'm a huge fan of the slow cooker.

The slow cooker can help you get a home-cooked meal on the table without any stress. My favourite recipes for the slow cooker have very few ingredients and minimal preparation time. You just put the ingredients in the slow cooker in the morning and let this incredible appliance slowly cook your meal all day long. Then when you're ready to eat, your dinner will be waiting for you!

In this opening chapter, I will discuss the benefits of using the slow cooker and I'll give you some of my best slow cooker tips and tricks. I'll also preview what's ahead in the recipes and tell you how to stock your pantry, so you'll be ready to start cooking. And I'll share some ideas on how to round out a meal.

The slow cooker uses an indirect heat source and doesn't scorch. You don't need to stir the food as you would if it were on a stove-top burner. The slow cooker uses moist heat to cook food, so don't lift the lid—every time you do, you release the steam surrounding and cooking the food.

Make sure to taste your food before serving. Because moisture does not evaporate in the slow cooker, flavours and spices can mellow and dissipate as time goes by. I often add seasonings right before serving slow-cooked food.

Slow cookers typically have just three settings: warm, low, and high, so they are easy to work with. All slow cookers cook differently. I have ten different slow cookers, and some cook faster than others. So, you will want to get to know your slow cooker.

There are several different sizes of slow cookers. All recipes were written using a 6-quart oval slow cooker in this book, which seems to be the most popular size.

If you are often away from home for several hours at a time, I suggest that you invest in a slow cooker with a timer on it. When you set the timer for the cooking time in the recipe, the slow cooker will switch to warm when the food is done and stay on warm (safely for up to 4 hours) until you can get home.

Don't reheat slow cooker leftovers in the slow cooker, because bacteria can grow in the time it takes for the food to reach a safe temperature.

I've learned the hard way not to place a hot slow cooker insert on a cold countertop or in a cold sink. The ceramic insert can crack if it is exposed to abrupt temperature shifts.

To remove stains in your slow cooker insert, simply fill it with water, add 1 cup of white vinegar, cover, and cook on high for 2 hours.

When you're shopping for a slow cooker, please keep in mind that there are appliances on the market referred to as slow cookers that have their heating element only on the bottom. Don't buy one of these to use for the recipes in this book.

Appliances with heating elements only on the bottom heat food more slowly than those with heating elements all around the insert. Experts do not recommend cooking large cuts of meat in this type of slow cooker (although it works for soups and stews). So when purchasing your slow cooker, please make sure it is a true one—with heating elements all around the insert.

Slow cookers typically have three settings: low, high, and warm. Most slow cookers set on low reach temperatures ranging from 85° to 95°C, depending on the individual slow cooker. On high, they reach temperatures between 120° and 150°C. So, when you are getting to know your slow cooker, regard the recipe cooking times as guidelines but not hard truths.

Caring for Your Slow Cooker

Your slow cooker's instruction manual contains the most pertinent information for caring for your slow cooker. Here are some basic tips:

- Try not to cook longer than the cooking time given in the recipe, so the food doesn't get burned.

- Do not add cold ingredients to a slow cooker that has already been heated. The insert is sensitive and may crack or break.

- Turn off, unplug and allow your slow cooker to cool down before cleaning.

- The heating base should not be submerged in water or any liquid.

- Always remove the lid first before removing the insert or stoneware.

The slow cooker insert is dishwasher safe. When using the dishwasher isn't enough, the following may be used:

- hot, soapy water

- baking soda (for gentle scrubbing)

- vinegar

Use a slow cooker liner or non-stick cooking spray to clean after cooking. Remember these simple tips and you'll be able to use your slow cooker for many meals and through many happy family occasions!

Why Use a Slow Cooker

- While the slow cooker isn't ideal for every cooking method, it does provide several major benefits by offering an effortless slow cooking experience. If you are planning to buy a slow cooker, keep reading to learn about some of the advantages of slow cooking.

- The lower cooking temperatures reduce the risk of burning the food items that tend to stick to the bottom of a pan or burn in an oven.

- Tough cheap meats, such as chuck steaks, roast, and less-lean stewing cattle, are tenderized by the long slow cooking.

- For many venison meals, the slow cooker is an ideal choice. The slow cooker keeps your oven and stovetop free for other cooking, and it's an excellent choice for large parties or holiday meals.

- Scrubbing many pots and pans is unnecessary. You'll only have to clean the slow cooker and a few prep items most of the time.

- Slow cookers consume less energy than conventional electric ovens.

- Unlike a huge oven, the slow cooker does not heat up the kitchen, which is a big bonus on a hot summer day.

- A slow cooker is easy to transport. It can be taken from the kitchen to the office or to a party. Simply plug it in and eat.

- A slow cooker can be easily left unattended all day. Before going to work, you can put the ingredients for a recipe in it and come home to supper. Whether you work from home or not, a slow cooker meal is a wonderful alternative for a hectic day.

Chapter 1
BREAKFAST RECIPES

Rice pudding with Jam

Prep Time: 5 minutes
Cooking Time: 3-4 hours
Servings: 4

Directions
1. Grease the inside of the slow cooker with butter then add the rice, milk, sugar and a little nutmeg if desired.
2. Stir gently, then cover with lid and cook using the Low setting for 3 to 4 hours, or until rice is tender and creamy.
3. Spread onto four plates and top with jam

Nutritions: Calories 184; Fat 9 g; Protein 6 g; Carbs 18 g; Fibre 0 g; Sugar 16 g

Ingredients
- 15g butter
- 100g pudding rice
- 750ml full-fat milk
- 25g caster sugar, ideally golden caster sugar
- ¼ tsp ground or grated nutmeg (optional)
- 4 heaped tbsp jam, to serve

Egg and Broccoli Casserole

Prep Time: 15 minutes
Cooking Time: 2½ to 3 hours
Servings: 6

Ingredients

- 700 g small-curd or natural cottage cheese
- 300 g frozen chopped broccoli, thawed and drained
- 450 g shredded Cheddar cheese
- 6 eggs, beaten
- 75 g flour
- 60 g butter, melted
- 3 tablespoons finely chopped onion
- ½ teaspoon salt
- Shredded cheese (optional)

Directions

1. Combine first 8 ingredients. Pour into greased slow cooker.
2. Cover and cook on high 1 hour. Stir. Reduce heat to low. Cover and cook 2½ to 3 hours, or until temperature reaches 70ºC and eggs are set.
3. Sprinkle with cheese and serve.

Nutritions: Calories 620; Fat 42 g; Protein 38 g; Carbs 18 g; Fibre 2 g; Sugar 4 g

Smoky Breakfast Casserole

Prep Time: 15 minutes
Cooking Time: 3 hours
Servings: 8 to 10

Directions
1. Mix together all ingredients together except for the Mozzarella cheese. Pour the mixture into greased slow cooker.
2. Now cover the top by sprinkling with Mozzarella cheese.
3. Cover with the lid and cook 2 hours on high, and then 1 hour on low.

Nutritions: Calories 562; Fat 46 g; Protein 29 g; Carbs 4 g; Fibre 0 g; Sugar 3 g

Ingredients
- 6 eggs, beaten
- 450 g little smokies (cocktail sausages), or 700 g sausages, browned and drained
- 375 ml milk
- 200 g shredded Cheddar cheese
- 8 slices bread, torn into pieces
- 1 teaspoon salt
- ½ teaspoon dry mustard
- 200 g shredded Mozzarella cheese

Hominy for Breakfast

Prep Time: 5 minutes
Cooking Time: 8 hours
Servings: 5

Ingredients
- 200 g dry cracked hominy or if unavailable, chickpeas, sweetcorn, buckwheat grits or polenta meal
- 1 teaspoon salt
- Black pepper (optional)
- 750 ml water
- 2 tablespoons butter

Directions
1. Stir all ingredients together in a greased slow cooker.
2. Cover and cook on low 8 hours, or overnight.
3. Serve warm for breakfast.

Nutritions: Calories 179; Fat 5 g; Protein 3 g; Carbs 31 g; Fibre 2 g; Sugar 0 g

Banana Bread for Breakfast

Prep Time: 15 minutes
Cooking Time: 3 hours
Servings: 6

Directions
1. In a bowl, combine the Weetabix with the sultanas, sugar and milk. Cover and let stand 10 minutes.
2. Line a 450g loaf pan with non-stick parchment paper. Pour boiled water into the slow cooker to a depth of about 5 cm. Preheat using the High setting while finishing the preparation of the cake.
3. Mash the banana in a bowl along with the eggs. Whisk together, then add to the soaked mixture with the flour, nutmeg, and salt. Stir well, then pour into the tin. Cover with greased aluminium foil and tuck well around the edges of the tin. Place in the slow cooker and cook using the High setting for 3 hours.
4. Using oven gloves, carefully lift the tin out of the slow cooker and check if the cake is cooked by inserting a toothpick, it should come out clean. Cook longer if needed.
5. Let cool on a wire rack, then slice and serve spread with mascarpone or low-fat soft cheese and topped with cranberries and honey.

Tip: You can serve as an afternoon tea treat, spread with butter, or just left plain.

Ingredients
- 3 packs of weetabix
- 80g of sultanas
- 120g of light brown sugar
- 200ml of milk
- 1 ripe banana
- 2 large eggs
- 120g of self-raising flour
- 1/4 tsp of grated nutmeg
- pinch of salt
- low fat soft cheese or mascarpone, blueberries and honey to serve

Nutritions: Calories 337; Fat 3 g; Protein 9 g; Carbs 69 g; Fibre 6 g; Sugar 19 g

Welsh Rarebit

Prep Time: 10 minutes
Cooking Time: 1½ to 2½ hours
Servings: 6 to 8

Directions
1. In slow cooker, combine beer, mustard, Worcestershire sauce, salt, and pepper. Cover and cook on high 1 to 2 hours, until mixture boils.
2. Add cheese, a little at a time, stirring constantly until all the cheese melts.
3. Heat on high 20 to 30 minutes with cover off, stirring frequently.
4. Serve hot over toasted English muffins or over toasted bread cut into triangles. Garnish with tomato slices, strips of crisp bacon and steamed asparagus spears.

Nutritions: Calories 567; Fat 46 g; Protein 33 g; Carbs 4 g; Fibre 0 g; Sugar 1 g

Ingredients
- 1 (330 ml) can beer
- 1 tablespoon dry mustard
- 1 teaspoon Worcestershire sauce
- ½ teaspoon salt
- ⅛ teaspoon black or white pepper
- 450 g processed cheese, cubed
- 450 g extra mature Cheddar cheese, cubed
- English muffins or toast
- Tomato slices
- Bacon, cooked until crisp
- Fresh steamed asparagus spears

Chapter 2
RED MEAT RECIPES

Easy Pulled Pork

Prep Time: 10 minutes
Cooking Time: 4-8 hours
Servings: 4

Directions

1. In a slow cooker, combine the tomato puree, paprika, orange juice and season with black pepper and salt. Add 4 tablespoons of cold water and stir well.
2. Put pork in the slow cooker and stir into the sauce several times until well coated. Cover with the lid and cook 4 to 5 hours on high or 6 to 8 hours on low setting until pork is very tender.
3. Break up the meat using two forks, then serve with buns and your favourite toppings

Nutritions: Calories 337; Fat 22 g; Protein 26 g; Carbs 4 g; Fibre 0 g; Sugar 3 g

Ingredients

For the pulled pork
- 3 tbsp tomato purée
- 1 tsp hot smoked paprika
- 2 oranges, juice only
- ½ tsp salt
- 4 pork shoulder steaks, or 600g boneless, pork shoulder joint, rind removed
- freshly ground black pepper

To serve
- 4 soft bread rolls, split in half
- 150g ready-made coleslaw
- 4 tbsp soured cream
- salad leaves

Lamb Osso Bucco

Prep Time: 15 minutes
Cooking Time: 4-8 hours
Servings: 4-6

Directions
1. Preheat the slow cooker. Season the lamb pieces and dust with flour. Heat 1 tablespoon of oil in a large pan. Sear the meat on all sides, then remove and place in the slow cooker.
2. Heat the remaining olive oil and add the carrots, onions, celery, garlic, thyme and a little salt and pepper.
3. Fry for 10 minutes, then add the wine, broth and tomatoes. Bring to the boil, then pour over the meat. Cover the slow cooker with the lid and cook using the High setting for 4 hours or using the Low one for 8 hours.
4. Meanwhile, mix the parsley, lemon and garlic in a bowl and sprinkle over the osso bucco before serving.

Nutritions: Calories 456; Fat 32 g; Protein 25.4 g; Carbs 19.2 g; Fibre 2.7 g; Sugar 7 g

Ingredients
- 800g lamb shoulder or leg meat cut into 5 cm pieces
- Flour, for dusting
- 5 tbsp olive oil
- 3 carrots diced
- 2 stalks celery diced
- 2 medium onions chopped
- 1 cloves garlic chopped
- 1 tsp fresh thyme, chopped
- 2 tin chopped tomatoes
- 200ml white wine
- 200ml beef stock
- For the gremolata
- 20g chopped flat leaf parsley
- zest of 1 lemon, plus extra to decorate
- 1 garlic clove, finely chopped

Easy chilli

Prep Time: 10 minutes
Cooking Time: 4-8 hours
Servings: 6

Directions
1. In a large non-stick frying pan, add the ground beef and onion and sear over medium-high heat, about 4 minutes. Give it a stir and use a couple of wooden spoons to press it against the sides of the pan to break up the ground beef as much as possible.
2. Add spices and cook 1 more minute; This quick process adds flavor depth. Pour the seasoned ground beef into the slow cooker and add the tomatoes, broth, tomato puree, and beans. Season with salt and black pepper. Cover with the lid and cook using the high setting for 4 to 5 hours or on low for 6 to 8 hours.
3. When done, serve the chili with your choice of freshly cooked rice, a dollop of sour cream, some coriander and a squeeze of fresh lime.

Nutritions: Calories 196; Fat 10 g; Protein 19 g; Carbs 4.5 g; Fibre 0.5 g; Sugar 1.5 g

Ingredients
- 400g tin chopped tomatoes
- 400g tin red kidney beans, drained and rinsed
- 500g beef mince
- 1 tsp hot smoked paprika
- 1 tsp ground cumin
- 1 tsp ground coriander
- 1 medium onion, finely chopped
- ½–1 tsp dried chilli flakes, or to taste
- 275 ml hot beef stock, made with 1 beef stock cube
- 3 tbsp tomato purée
- salt and freshly ground black pepper

For serving
- rice, soured cream, coriander and lime wedges (optional)

Beef Stew Easy Recipe

Prep Time: 10 minutes
Cooking Time: 8-10 hours
Servings: 6

Directions
1. Pour the boiled water into a heatproof measuring jug, add broth cube, tomato puree and yeast extract. Stir well until the cube has dissolved and set aside.
2. Place the meat, bacon and vegetables in a slow cooker, sprinkle over the flour and season with the salt, herbs and ground black pepper.
3. Mix. Add the broth and stir well.
4. Cover with lid and cook using the Low setting until meat and vegetables are tender, 8 to 10 hours.
5. Serve beef stew with mashed potatoes.

Nutritions: Calories 624; Fat 42 g; Protein 44 g; Carbs 11 g; Fibre 2 g; Sugar 4 g

Ingredients
- 600ml just-boiled water
- 1 beef stock cube
- 2 tbsp tomato purée
- 1 tbsp yeast extract
- 900g good-quality braising steak, trimmed and cut into roughly 4cm chunks
- 100g smoked bacon lardons, or sliced smoked back bacon
- 2 onions, thinly sliced
- 4 carrots (about 400g), peeled and cut into roughly 3 cm pieces
- 4 celery sticks, trimmed and cut into 3 cm lengths
- 3 tbsp plain flour (25g)
- 1 tsp of flaked sea salt, plus extra to season
- 1 tsp dried mixed herbs
- 1 bay leaf (dried or fresh)
- ground black pepper
- mashed potatoes, to serve

Pork shoulder with butterbeans, apple, and sage

Prep Time: lass then 30 minutes
Cooking Time: 7 hours
Servings: 4

Ingredients
- 2 onions, roughly chopped
- 2 sticks celery, thinly sliced
- small bunch fresh sage
- salt and freshly ground black pepper
- 2 x 400g cans butterbeans in water, rinsed and drained
- 4 thick pork shoulder steaks
- 1 tbsp olive oil
- 400ml dry cider
- 100ml strong, good quality chicken stock
- 30g butter
- 1 apple, peeled
- 1 tsp cornflour mixed with 1 tbsp cold water until smooth
- 2 tbsp wholegrain mustard

Directions
1. In a slow cooker, place the onions, celery, and chopped sage leaves, then season with salt and black pepper. Scatter with the butterbeans.
2. Season the meat with salt and black pepper. Heat the oil in a non-stick pan, then fry the pork on both sides until golden brown. Place in the slow cooker.
3. Add the cider and broth to the same pan and bring to a boil. Pour over the meat then cover the slow cooker with the lid and cook using the low setting for 7 hours. The pork should be tender and surrounded with sauce.
4. Cut the apple into eight wedges throwing away the core. Heat the butter in a pan, then add the apple and sauté until golden-brown and tender, 8-10 minutes. Add about 15 more sage leaves, increase heat and sauté until leaves are crisp.
5. Remove the pork from the slow cooker and arrange on a serving platter. Mix the cornflour paste and mustard with the beans in the slow cooker and stir until the sauce thickens a little. Top the pork with the beans sauce, apple and crisp fried sage.

Nutritions: Calories 501; Fat 32 g; Protein 40 g; Carbs 12 g; Fibre 1 g; Sugar 2 g

Massaman Curry

Prep Time: 20-25 minutes
Cooking Time: 8 hours
Servings: 4

Directions
1. Place the potatoes in the slow cooker.
2. Heat a large non-stick pan and sear the meat in batches until golden brown, then place in the slow cooker. There is no need to add oil to the pan as the meat is quite fatty.
3. Add the masaman paste, coriander stalks and ginger to the pan and sauté for a few minutes until fragrant.
4. Add the coconut milk and bring to the boil.
5. Season to taste with the sugar, lime zest and fish sauce, adding lime leaves if desired, then pour the sauce over the meat and potatoes. Cover the slow cooker with it's lid and cook on low setting for 8 hours until very tender.
6. Remove excess fat from curry, add the juice from half the zested lime and add more fish sauce if needed. The curry should have a balanced mix of sour, salty, hot and sweet, without one flavour dominating.
7. Sprinkle with coriander leaves and peanuts, then serve with the rice and the remaining lime in wedges, for squeezing

Nutritions: Calories 860; Fat 66 g; Protein 38 g; Carbs 27 g; Fibre 4 g; Sugar 4 g

Ingredients
- 800-850g boned lamb shoulder or beef shin, cut into matchbox-size pieces
- 3 tbsp massaman curry paste
- small bunch fresh coriander, stalks finely chopped
- 5cm piece fresh root ginger, finely grated
- 400ml coconut milk
- 500g new potatoes, halved
- 6 freeze-dried kaffir lime leaves (optional)
- 1 tsp light muscovado sugar
- 1 lime, zest and juice
- 1 tbsp fish sauce (you can add extra if you desider)
- handful roasted unsalted peanuts, roughly chopped, for serving

Prep Time: less than 30 minutes
Cooking Time: 9 hours
Servings: 6

Ingredients

- 1–2 tbsp olive oil
- 1.2kg beef brisket joint
- 2 onions, halved
- 1.4kg medium–large, floury potatoes, such as Maris Piper
- 5 carrots, peeled and trimmed
- 4 tbsp cornflour
- 1 tbsp dried mixed herbs (if you prefer herbes de provence)
- 1 tsp English mustard powder
- 1 tbsp tomato purée
- 1 tbsp Worcestershire sauce
- 1 tbsp yeast extract
- 170ml red wine (or beef stock, same quantity)
- 1 beef stock pot
- 1 litre boiling water
- salt and freshly ground black pepper
- 900g mixed green vegetables, cooked, to serve

Roast beef in Slow Cooker

Directions

1. Preheat the slow cooker using the low setting.
2. Place a large, heavy-bottomed skillet over high heat. Rub the entire brisket with oil, then season well with salt and pepper. Fry on all sides in the pan until well browned. Now you can lift the brisket into to the slow cooker.
3. Put the onion halves into the holes around the meat, then place the potatoes and finally the carrots on top and around.
4. Put the kettle on.
5. In a measuring jug, combine half the cornflour, herb mix, and mustard. Using a fork, mash inside the jug the tomato purée, followed by the Worcestershire sauce and the yeast extract. Slowly pour in the red wine until you have a smooth paste and all of the wine is incorporated.
6. Add the beef stock and then add the boiling water to the jug. Pour this mixture over the meat and vegetables, cover the slow cooker with the lid and cook for 9 hours. The meat and vegetables should be very tender.
7. Carefully lift the meat, carrots, and potatoes onto a platter and cover with aluminum foil to keep warm. Pour the rest in a large saucepan and bring to a boil.
8. Mix a small amount of the gravy with the remaining cornflour to form a smooth paste then whisk it back into the saucepan.
9. Simmer until reduced by about a third. At this stage you can discard the onions or, if you like them, slice and mix with the other vegetables.
10. Use two forks to break the beef into large chunks and discard any leftover fat.
11. Push the meat to one side of the plate and set the veggies alongside , cutting the potatoes in halfs.
12. Adjust the gravy with salt and pepper, and pour some over the meat and veggies.

Nutritions: Calories 585; Fat 17 g; Protein 43 g; Carbs 60 g; Fibre 11 g; Sugar 5 g

Chinese-style Beef

Prep Time: 15 minutes
Cooking Time: 4 hours
Servings: 4

Ingredients
- 2 tbsp sunflower oil
- 2 large red onions, thinly sliced
- 50g piece fresh root ginger, peeled, finely grated
- 4 garlic cloves, crushed
- 1 tsp dried chilli flakes
- 500g braising steak, trimmed, cut into 5cm cubes
- 2 tsp Chinese five-spice powder
- 350ml hot beef stock (made with 1 stock cube)
- 4 tbsp dark soy sauce
- 4 tsp cornflour
- 2 tbsp clear honey
- freshly ground black pepper

Directions
1. Heat the oil in a large, heavy-bottomed frying pan over medium-high heat. Add the onions and sauté for 8-10 minutes, stirring regularly, until soft and lightly browned. Now you can add the ginger, garlic and chilli flakes. Stir well and cook for 2-3 minutes, be careful to not burn the garlic.
2. Season the meat with pepper, then sprinkle the five spices powder on top. Add to the pan and fry for 3-4 minutes, turning the meat regularly, until lightly browned on all sides.
3. Add to the slow cooker. Pour in the broth and add the soy sauce. Cover and cook on high setting until the meat is tender, about 4 hours.
4. When the meat is cooked, stir together cornflour with 1 tablespoon water and add the honey. Pour in the slow cooker, cover with the lid and cook 12 to 15 minutes, or until sauce is glossy and slightly thickened.
5. You can serve beef with steamed rice, boiled noodles, and stir-fried vegetables.

Nutritions: Calories 311; Fat 22 g; Protein 23 g; Carbs 3 g; Fibre 0 g; Sugar 1 g

Lamb Rogan Josh

Prep Time: less than 12 minutes
Cooking Time: 4-8 hours
Servings: 4

Directions
1. Heat up the slow cooker using the High setting.
2. Put the chopped onions and the curry paste in a food processor with 100 ml of water and pulse until smooth.
3. Place in the slow cooker, then add thinly sliced onion, lamb chunks, cumin, cinnamon, and bay leaves.
4. Use kitchen scissors to cut the plum tomatoes into small pieces and then tip them into the slow cooker. Stir everything well, season with salt and pepper and cover with the lid. Cook 4 hours on high or 8 to 9 hours on low until lamb is tender but not dry. If you wanto to use the pepper, add it during the last hour of cooking.
5. Add the yoghurt and leave for 10 minutes before serving.
6. Serve with rice or your choice of serving options.

Nutritions: Calories 274; Fat 12 g; Protein 31 g; Carbs 8 g; Fibre 1 g; Sugar 6 g

Ingredients
- 2 onions, 1½ roughly chopped, ½ thinly sliced
- 100g rogan josh spice paste (or follow pack guidance for serving 4 people)
- 600g lamb neck fillet or shoulder, excess fat trimmed and diced into 3–4 cm pieces
- 1 tsp cumin seeds
- A cinnamon stick
- 2 fresh or dried bay leaves
- 400g of tin plum tomatoes
- 1 pepper of any colour cutted into big chunks (optional)
- 110g of yoghurt (full-fat Greek-style or plain)
- salt and ground black pepper
- cooked rice to serve

Beef Hotpot

Prep Time: 20 minutes
Cooking Time: 8 hours
Servings: 6

Ingredients
- 1 onion, chopped
- 2 carrots, cut into 1cm slices
- 1 tbsp vegetable or sunflower oil
- 500g beef brisket, trimmed of excess fat and cut into matchbox-size cubes, or long, thick slices
- 4 garlic cloves, crushed or finely chopped
- 5cm piece fresh root ginger, finely grated
- 1 fat red chilli, shredded (you can leave the seeds in or not. Its up to you)
- 2 tbsp of light muscovado sugar
- 1 tbsp of miso paste (optional but highly recommended)
- 6 tbsp light soy sauce
- 300 ml of beef stock
- 1 tsp of sesame oil, plus more for serving
- 1-2 bunches spring onions, trimmed then cut into finger-length pieces
- few handfuls fresh beansprouts

Directions
1. Place the onion and carrots in the slow cooker.
2. Heat the oil in a large non-stick frying pan, then fry the meat in two batches until golden brown, then add to the slow cooker. Sprinkle with garlic, ginger, and chili.
3. Stir the sugar, miso, soybeans, broth, and sesame oil with the meat's juices in the pan, then bring to a simmer and stir to dissolve the miso and sugar.
4. Pour hot liquid over meat and vegetables, cover with lid and cook on low setting for 7½ hours.
5. Sprinkle with the spring onions, cover the slow cooker again and cook for another 30 minutes until the onions are soft.
6. Add the beansprouts and drizzle with a little more sesame oil. Serve with steamed broccoli and rice.

Nutritions: Calories 174; Fat 8 g; Protein 18 g; Carbs 4 g; Fibre 0 g; Sugar 1 g

Barbecue-style Pork Chops

Prep Time: 10 minutes
Cooking Time: 8-10 hours
Servings: 4

Directions
1. In the slow cooker, combine tomatoes, honey, ketchup, soy sauce, and smoked paprika until well combined. Season with ground black pepper.
2. Add the pork and turn so that it is soaked in the sauce. Cover and cook using the low setting for 8 to 10 hours, or until sauce is thick and glossy and pork is tender.
3. You can serve with cooked rice and corn on the cob, if desired

Nutritions: Calories 345; Fat 18 g; Protein 30 g; Carbs 13 g; Fibre 1 g; Sugar 12 g

Ingredients
- 400g can chopped tomatoes
- 4 tbsp clear honey
- 2 tbsp tomato ketchup
- 2 tbsp dark soy sauce
- ½ tsp hot smoked paprika
- 4 thick pork chops (each about 170g)
- ground black pepper
- boiled rice
- cooked corn on the cob (optional)

Prep Time: overnight
Cooking Time: 7-9 hours
Servings: 4

Ingredients

- 3 tbsp olive oil
- 1kg braising or stewing beef, cut into chunks
- 2 tbsp plain flour
- 1½ tbsp mild paprika (not smoked)
- 2 onions, chopped
- 1 garlic cloves, crushed
- 2 peppers, any colour, cut into bite-sized chunks
- 350g tin chopped tomatoes
- 3 tbsp tomato purée
- 1 tsp caraway seeds (optional)
- 1 beef stock cube, crumbled
- 1 tsp caster or granulated sugar
- salt and black pepper
- ½ small bunch curly or flatleaf parsley, chopped, to garnish
- 9-10 tbsp soured cream, to serve

Goulash in Slow Cooker

Directions

1. Brown the meat the night before or in the morning to get more flavour. Heat 2 tablespoons oil in a large frying pan over medium-high heat and sear the meat in batches until the pieces are seared and browned on all sides.
2. Remove the meat and place it in a bowl. Pour 200 ml of water into the same pan and cook over low heat, scraping all pieces of meat from the bottom. Pour into a jug.
3. Stir the flour and paprika into the pieces of meat. Return to pan with remaining oil and cook, stirring, for 2 minutes until dustiness has disappeared. If making it the night before, cool the meat to room temperature and then refrigerate overnight with the jug of stock.
4. To cook the goulash, add the meat chunks, onions, garlic, and peppers into the slow cooker. Pour the tomatoes into a large jug or bowl and mix with the tomato puree, caraway seeds if using, crumbled stock cube and sugar.
5. Pour 450ml of water into the reserved broth and pour this mixture and tomato mixture over the meat and vegetables. Give everything a good stir.
6. Cook using the low setting until the meat is tender and the sauce has slightly thickened, 7-9 hours. Season with salt and pepper and mix with half the parsley.
7. To serve, stir the sour cream and garnish with the remaining parsley and a little black pepper.

Nutritions: Calories 889; Fat 56 g; Protein 75 g; Carbs 14 g; Fibre 2 g; Sugar 5 g

Sausage and Lentil Casserole

Prep Time: 15 minutes
Cooking Time: 4-8 hours
Servings: 4

Ingredients
- spray oil
- 350g pork chipolata sausages (about 12 sausages)
- 1 bulb fennel, finely sliced, leafy fronds reserved for garnish
- 200g dried green lentils
- 700ml chicken stock
- 2 bay leaves (optional)
- large pinch fennel seeds, ground
- 2 small onions, thinly sliced
- 1 fat garlic clove, crushed
- 125ml dry white wine

Directions
1. If necessary, preheat your slow cooker.
2. Heat some cooking spray in a pan over high heat. Once hot, add the sausages and saute' until golden then transfer to the slow cooker.
3. Meanwhile, add the fennel, lentils, chicken broth, bay leaves (if using), and fennel seeds to the slow cooker.
4. Sauté the onions, in the same pan of the sausage, until softened. Add the garlic and fry for a minute. Increase the heat and add the wine, allow to simmer for a minute, then pour the ingredients into the slow cooker.
5. Season with salt and pepper and stir.
6. Cover with the lid and cook using the high setting for 4 hours or using the low one for 7 to 8 hours. Serve in hot bowls and garnish with the reserved fennel leaves.

Nutritions: Calories 442; Fat 31 g; Protein 21 g; Carbs 14 g; Fibre 0 g; Sugar 1 g

Beef Brisket with Bean Mash

Prep Time: 20 minutes
Cooking Time: 8-10 hours
Servings: 4

Directions
1. Season the meat with black pepper and salt according to your taste.
2. Sprinkle the sliced onions and bay leaves over the bottom of the slow cooker, place the brisket on top and pour over the stout. Cook on low setting for 8-10 hours.
3. For the bean puree, heat the butter in a pan and cook the leeks over very low heat, around 20 minutes or until tender.
4. Add the garlic and thyme leaves and season with salt and black pepper.
5. Place the beans, leek mixture, crème fraîche, parsley, and puree in a food processor or blender.
6. Pour the beans and leek mixture back into the pan and heat well. Season to taste with salt and black pepper.
7. To serve, transfer the puree to serving plates. Slice the meat and place alongside spooning some of the cooking liquid form the slow cooker on top

Nutritions: Calories 700; Fat 34 g; Protein 86 g; Carbs 10 g; Fibre 0 g; Sugar 1 g

Ingredients

For the beef brisket
- 1.5kg beef brisket joint
- salt and freshly ground black pepper
- 2 onions, thinly sliced
- 3 fresh bay leaves
- 350ml Irish stout

For the cannellini bean mash
- knob of butter
- 3 leeks, white parts only, thinly sliced
- 1or 2 garlic cloves (as you prefer)
- few sprigs fresh thyme, leaves only, or ½ tsp dried thyme
- 2 x 400g tins cannellini beans
- 4 tbsp crème fraîche
- 1 tbsp chopped fresh parsley (optional)

Chapter 3

POULTRY RECIPES

Chicken Korma

Prep Time: 10 minutes
Cooking Time: 3-6 hours
Servings: 4–5

Directions
1. Heat up the slow cooker turning it to the High setting.
2. Place the onions, curry paste, turmeric and almonds in a food processor. Add 100ml of water and mix until the paste is very smooth. Scrape the mixture into the slow cooker.
3. Stir the chicken pieces into the curry mixture.
4. Add another 200ml water and cook using the Low setting for 6 hours or the High one for 3 hours, until the chicken is really tender and the sauce is thick and golden.
5. Add the cream and sultanas, if using, and cook on high for a further 15 minutes.
6. Flavour the curry with salt and pepper. Sprinkle with the flaked almonds you set aside and serve with rice or bread.

Nutritions: Calories 778; Fat 75 g; Protein 17 g; Carbs 7 g; Fibre 1 g; Sugar 3 g

Ingredients
- 2 small–medium onions, roughly chopped
- 100g korma curry paste (or follow pack guidance for serving 4–5 people)
- 2 tsp ground turmeric
- 40g flaked almonds, plus 2 tbsp to garnish (toasted if preferred)
- 8 small chicken thighs (about 700–750g) skin removed, boneless, excess fat trimmed and each thigh cut into 3–5 pieces
- 100ml of double cream or Greek-style yoghurt
- handful sultanas or raisins (optional)
- salt and ground black pepper
- basmati rice and/or warmed naan bread, to serve

Spring Chicken and Herb Soup

Prep Time: 15 minutes
Cooking Time: 6 hours
Servings: 8

Ingredients
- 4 large chicken thighs, bone in, skin and extra fat removed
- 2 onions, roughly chopped
- 1 tsp English mustard powder
- 2 chicken stock pots (or stock cubes)
- 2 tbsp wholegrain mustard
- 2 bay leaves
- 2.5 litres boiling water
- 300g baby Chantenay carrots, scrubbed and larger ones halved
- 125g pearl barley
- 200g frozen peas
- 200g frozen broad beans
- 15g fresh flatleaf parsley, finely chopped
- 10g fresh tarragon, finely chopped
- 10g fresh chives, finely snipped
- ½ lemon, juice only
- salt and freshly ground black pepper

Directions
1. Heat up the slow cooker turning it to the Low setting and bring a kettle to the boil.
2. Add the chicken thighs and onions to the slow cooker with the dry mustard, pots, whole grain mustard and bay leaves. Pour boiling water on, cover and cook for 5 hours on Low setting.
3. Add the carrots and pearl barley. Cook for another hour until the carrots and barley are soft.
4. Turn off the slow cooker and remove the chicken. Remove and discard the bay leaves and add the peas and beans. Cover again.
5. Crumble the chicken meat from the bones into small pieces. Stir the chicken, herbs and lemon juice in the slow cooker again and season with salt and pepper.
6. Serve straight into bowls or allow to cool to room temperature before refrigerating and reheating over the next day or two

Nutritions: Calories 533; Fat 44 g; Protein 13 g; Carbs 19 g; Fibre 4 g; Sugar 3 g

Chicken Cacciatore in Slow Cooker

Prep Time: 5 minutes
Cooking Time: 3-6 hours
Servings: 6

Directions
1. Heat up the slow cooker turning it to the High setting. Add all the ingredients seasosing with fresh black pepper and a pinch of salt.
2. Cook 3 hours on High setting or 6 hours on Low until chicken is really tender. During cooking, the meat should have broken into smaller pieces, but if not, break the thighs into pieces with a spoon.
3. Serve with pasta, potatoes or polenta with cheese and green vegetables or a salad.

Nutritions: Calories 516; Fat 45 g; Protein 12 g; Carbs 15 g; Fibre 2.5 g; Sugar 6 g

Ingredients
- 2 onions, finely chopped
- 2 celery sticks, finely chopped
- 6 garlic cloves, sliced
- 6 large chicken thighs, skin removed and boneless
- 2 red, orange or yellow peppers, cut into big chunks
- 2 x 400g tins chopped tomatoes
- 150ml of chicken stock, made with 1 stock cube
- 2 tsp dried basil
- 1 tbsp sugar
- 1 tbsp wine or balsamic vinegar
- 75g olives, stones removed and drained salt and freshly ground black pepper

To serve
- freshly cooked pasta, potatoes or cheesy polenta
- freshly cooked green vegetables or salad

Prep Time: overnight
Cooking Time: 3-6 hours
Servings: 6–8

Ingredients

- 1–1.2kg, about 10–11 chicken thighs, boneless and without skin
- 4 garlic cloves, crushed
- 1 large lemon, juice only
- 3 tbsp olive oil
- 3 large onions, very thickly sliced into rounds
- few pinches dried oregano
- salt and black pepper

For the spice mix

- 2 tsp ground cumin
- 2 tsp ground coriander
- 2 tsp paprika (plain or sweet smoked)
- 2 tsp turmeric
- ½ tsp black pepper
- ½ tsp cayenne pepper
- 2 tsp onion granules (optional)
- 1 tsp salt

To serve

- warmed pitta, flatbread or wraps
- chopped salad ingredients
- tzatziki, hummus, garlic or chilli sauces
- pickled turnips and chilli

Chicken shawarma in Slow Cooker

Directions
1. Marine the chicken overnight for best results. Combine the spice mix ingredients in a food bag or bowl, then sprinkle the spices over the chicken thighs. Using your hands, massage the spices all over the meat. Cover and leave in the fridge overnight or as long as you can.
2. Preheat the slow cooker using the High setting.
3. In a jug, whisk together the garlic, lemon juice, and olive oil with a fork. Drizzle some into the bottom of the slow cooker, then add the chicken. Try to place the thighs at angles to fit in snugly and to create an even layer with no gaps. Drizzle the remaining lemon oil on top. Cook 6 hours using the Low setting or 3 hours using the High one, until chicken is falling apart and still juicy.
4. Turn off the slow cooker and preheat the grill. Arrange the onions on a baking sheet, brush the top with some juice from the slow cooker, season with salt and pepper and sprinkle with half the oregano. Turn the onions and repeat. Grill 2 to 4 minutes on each side until onions are well charred.
5. Use two forks to shred chicken.
6. Place the shredded chicken in the warmed pitas with the grilled onions, salads, sauces and pickles.

Nutritions: Calories 599; Fat 60 g; Protein 12 g; Carbs 2 g; Fibre 0 g; Sugar 1 g

Honey Mustard Chicken

Prep Time: 10 minutes
Cooking Time: 3-4 hours
Servings: 4

Ingredients
- 1 tsp of oil (sunflower, vegetable or light olive oil)
- 6–8 chicken thighs, with skin and bone-in
- 300 ml of hot chicken stock, made with 1 stock cube
- 2 tbsp of mustard (English, wholegrain or a combination)
- 2 tbsp of honey
- ½ tsp of dried mixed herbs
- 4 tbsp of double cream
- 1 tbsp of cornflour mixed with 1 tbsp of cold water
- salt and freshly ground black pepper

1. Season the chicken with salt and black pepper then heat the oil in a large non-stick pan over medium-high heat.
2. Cook the chicken thighs, skin-side down, for 3-5 minutes or until crispy and golden brown. Flip and fry the other side for 2 minutes. Frying gives the chicken a nice color and removes some of the fat just under the skin
3. While the chicken is cooking, pour the stock into the slow cooker and add the mustard, honey, and herbs mixing well.
4. Place the chicken with the skin-side up in the slow cooker, cover with the lid and cook using the High setting for 3 to 4 hours.
5. Once the chicken is cooked through, carefully add the heavy cream and cornflour mixture, cover and cook an additional 10 minutes or until the sauce thickens. (If your chicken has released lots of fat into the pot, it's better to spoon a little off before adding the cream.)
6. You can serve the chicken hot with the sauce and plenty of freshly cooked vegetables with potatoes or rice on the side.

Nutritions: Calories 966; Fat 92 g; Protein 21 g; Carbs 11 g; Fibre 0 g; Sugar 9 g

Chicken Tacos

Prep Time: 10 minutes
Cooking Time: 5-7 hours
Servings: 4–6

Directions
1. In the slow cooker, add ketchup, honey, Worcestershire sauce, orange juice, paprika, and garlic. Season with salt and ground black pepper and mix well.
2. Add the chicken thighs, turning to coat with the sauce. Move the thighs away from the sides of the pot to prevent them from sticking as the sauce reduces.
3. Cover with the lid and cook using the Low setting for 5 to 7 hours or until the chicken is tender.
4. Using two forks, shred the chicken while mixing it with the sauce. Note that the sauce will thicken the longer the chicken cooks, so ladle a little out before shredding the chicken if cooking for the shorter time.
5. To serve, spoon the chicken with the sour cream, fresh cilantro, and lime juice into warm mini tortillas.

Nutritions: Calories 709; Fat 66 g; Protein 14 g; Carbs 14 g; Fibre 0 g; Sugar 12 g

Ingredients
- 100g tomato ketchup
- 4 tbsp runny honey
- 3 tbsp Worcestershire sauce
- 70 ml of orange juice (see tip)
- 1 tsp of hot smoked paprika
- 1 garlic cloves, thinly sliced, or 1 tsp of garlic granules
- 6–8 chicken thighs, boneless and skinless
- salt and black pepper
- To serve
- flour tortillas, coriander, lime wedges and soured cream

Butter Chicken

Prep Time: 5 minutes
Cooking Time: 4-5 hours
Servings: 4

Ingredients
- 20 g of butter, cut into small pieces
- 4 garlic cloves, finely grated (according to your taste)
- 20 g of chunk root ginger, peeled and grated
- 4 tsp of medium curry powder
- ¼ tsp of chilli flakes
- 2 tbsp of tomato purée
- 1 tbsp of caster sugar
- 8 boneless, skinless chicken thighs, cutted into 4 similar sized pieces
- 100 ml of double cream
- salt and freshly ground black

Directions
1. Add the butter, garlic, ginger, curry powder, chili flakes, tomato puree and sugar to the slow cooker and mix well.
2. Add the chicken, seasoned with salt and pepper and toss with the spice mixture, until all sides are covered. Add 75ml cold water and stir well.
3. Cover with the lid and cook using the High setting for 4 to 5 hours, until the chicken is very tender.
4. Add the cream to the slow cooker, cover with the lid again and cook using the High setting for a further 10 minutes
5. Adjust the seasonings as you like and serve with freshly cooked rice and fresh coriander

Nutritions: Calories 953; Fat 73 g; Protein 64 g; Carbs 3 g; Fibre 0 g; Sugar 2 g

Chapter 4

VEGETARIAN RECIPES

Harissa Vegetable Stew

Prep Time: 5 minutes
Cooking Time: 3-6 hours
Servings: 8

Ingredients
- 400g of parsnips, trimmed, peeled, woody core removed and cut into short batons
- 2 onions cut into very thin wedges (red, white or a mixture)
- 5 large carrots, peeled and cut into 2cm slices
- 2 x 400g tins butterbeans (or other white beans)
- 2 tbsp of harissa
- 1 tbsp of dried oregano or mixed herbs
- 1 tbsp of honey
- 400g tin chopped tomatoes
- 400ml of vegetable stock
- 2 tbsp tomato purée
- about 100g kale, thick stalks discarded and roughly chopped
- salt and freshly ground black pepper

Directions
1. Preheat the slow cooker turning it on the High setting. Add parsnips, onions and carrots.
2. Drain one tins of beans and pour them into the slow cooker along with the other tin of beans(use the liquid too). Add harissa, oregano, honey, chopped tomatoes, broth, and tomato puree. Season with salt and pepper and stir.
3. Cook using the high setting for 3-4 hours or using the low one for 5-6 hours until vegetables are really tender.
4. Add kale, cover slow cooker with lid and leave to soften for 5 minutes. Adjust the flavour with salt and pepper and serve with couscous, rice or fried potatoes and dollops of yoghurt.

Nutritions: Calories 893; Fat 38 g; Protein 55 g; Carbs 82 g; Fibre 29 g; Sugar 8 g

Aloo gobi in Slow Cooker

Prep Time: 5 minutes
Cooking Time: 3 hours
Servings: 4

Directions
1. Preheat the slow cooker turning it on the High setting. If you want to use the cumin and nigella seeds, toast them in a small pan until fragrant (around 1 minute) then add to slow cooker with the remaining ingredients and ½ teaspoon salt.
2. Cook using the Low setting for 3 hours, potatoes should be tender. Adjust flavour with salt and pepper and serve with rice or naan bread, yoghurt and cauliflower leaves, if desired.

Nutritions: Calories 213; Fat 8 g; Protein 4 g; Carbs 30 g; Fibre 4 g; Sugar 6 g

Ingredients
- 1½ tsp of cumin seeds
- 2 tsp of nigella seeds (optional)
- 4 large garlic cloves, crushed
- 1 tbsp of grated fresh root ginger (or ginger purée)
- 500g tomatoes, chopped (or 400g tin chopped tomatoes)
- 4 tsp mild curry powder
- 2 tsp turmeric
- 3 tbsp butter or ghee
- 1 tbsp tomato purée
- 500g of new potatoes, halved or quartered
- 1 cauliflower, head chopped into small florets and leaves saved
- salt and freshly ground black pepper

To serve
- freshly cooked rice or warmed naan bread
- plain yoghurt

Veggie-Style Bolognese

Prep Time: 7 minutes
Cooking Time: 4-8 hours
Servings: 4

Ingredients
- 2 tbsp of oil (sunflower, vegetable or light olive oil)
- 1 medium onion, finely chopped
- 2 garlic cloves, crushed
- 2–3 medium carrots, about 200g, peeled and cut into small chunks
- 200g mushrooms, any kind, sliced
- 2 x 400 g tins of green lentils, drained and rinsed
- 400g tin chopped tomatoes
- 150 ml of hot vegetable stock, made with 1 stock cube
- 3 tbsp tomato purée
- 2 tsp caster sugar
- 1 tsp dried oregano
- 2 dried bay leaves, or 1 fresh
- salt and freshly ground black pepper
- freshly cooked pasta, grated cheese and basil, to serve (optional)

Directions
1. In a large nonstick pan, heat the oil and sauté the onion over medium-high heat stirring regularly, about 3 minutes
2. Add the garlic and fry for 1 more minute.
3. Transfer the onion and garlic mixture in the slow cooker along with the carrots, mushrooms, lentils, tomatoes, broth, tomato puree, sugar and herbs.
4. Season with salt and black pepper.
5. Cover with the lid and cook using the High setting for 4-5 hours or on low for 6-8 hours.
6. Serve with fresh pasta, grated cheese and fresh basil, if desired.

Nutritions: Calories 344; Fat 8 g; Protein 19 g; Carbs 59 g; Fibre 4 g; Sugar 7 g

Dhal in Slow Cooker

Prep Time: 10 minutes
Cooking Time: 4 hours
Servings: 4

Directions
1. In a slow cooker, combine peas, onion, tomatoes, ginger, ground cumin, turmeric, crushed garlic, curry leaves and broth. Add most of the chili and mix well.
2. Cook using the High setting for four hours, until the peas are tender. Season the dhal generously with salt and freshly ground black pepper.
3. Just before serving, heat the oil in a saucepan.
4. Once the oil is hot, add the whole cumin and chopped garlic. Fry until the garlic is golden brown and the cumin smells almost smoky.
5. Spoon hot spice oil over dhal, sprinkle with remaining green chili and serve with lemon wedges for squeezing.

Nutritions: Calories 345; Fat 7 g; Protein 18 g; Carbs 52 g; Fibre 19 g; Sugar 9 g

Ingredients
- 300g yellow split peas
- 1 onion, chopped
- 200g of tomatoes, chopped (from a tin or fresh)
- A thumb of fresh root ginger, grated
- 2 tsp of cumin seeds, 1 tsp crushed finely in a mortar
- 2 tsp of ground turmeric
- 2 garlic cloves, one crushed, one thinly sliced
- 8-9 freeze-dried curry leaves
- 650ml hot vegetable stock
- 1 hot green finger chilli, thinly sliced
- 2 tbsp vegetable or sunflower oil
- lemon wedges, to serve

Butternut Squash Mac & Cheese

Prep Time: 15 minutes
Cooking Time: 4 hours
Servings: 6

Ingredients
- 500g macaroni or other short pasta
- 350g butternut squash (cubed)
- 200ml vegetable broth
- 150g shredded sharp cheddar cheese
- 150g grated gouda or gruyere cheese
- 150ml milk
- 1 garlic clove
- 1 onion
- ¼ tsp red pepper flakes
- ¼ tsp thyme
- 100g grated parmesan cheese (optional)

Directions
1. Mince the garlic and dice the onion.
2. Heat olive oil in a frying pan over medium heat. Cook the garlic and onion for 2-3 minutes until fragrant and tender then add them to the slow cooker followed by the broth and cubed butternut squash. Stir together.
3. Cover with the lid and cook using the high setting for 4 hours.
4. About 10-15 minutes before cooking time is complete, start making the pasta. Bring a pot of water to boil and cook the pasta till they're al dente.
5. Once the squash is cooked and tender, use a blender or potato masher to create a smooth paste.
6. Add the shredded cheese and milk. Season with salt, pepper, thyme, and red pepper flakes. Stir to fully combine.
7. Add the cooked pasta to the cheesy squash sauce.
8. Serve with grated parmesan cheese.

Nutritions: Calories 605; Fat 21 g; Protein 31 g; Carbs 74 g; Fibre 4 g

Veggie Slow Cooker Curry

Prep Time: less than 30 mins
Cooking Time: over 2 hours
Servings: 4

Directions
1. In a frying pan, heat the oil and sauté the onion, stirring frequently, for 5 minutes or until lightly browned. Add the garlic and curry paste and cook for a further 30 seconds, stirring constantly.
2. Place in the slow cooker and add the butternut squash and carrot.
3. Sprinkle over the flour and mix.
4. Add tomatoes, chickpeas, frozen spinach, sugar and broth.
5. Stir well, cover the slow cooker with the lid and cook using the Low setting for 9-11 hours or until vegetables are tender and spices have mellowed.
6. Stir well before serving with freshly cooked basmati rice, yoghurt and various chutneys and pickles

Nutritions: Calories 540; Fat 9 g; Protein 24 g; Carbs 92 g; Fibre 17 g; Sugar 19 g

Ingredients
- 2 tbsp sunflower oil
- 1 onion, thinly sliced
- 1 garlic cloves, very thinly sliced
- 2 tbsp Indian medium curry paste
- 3 tbsp plain flour
- 500g butternut squash, peeled and cut into roughly 2cm chunks
- 1 carrot, peeled, halved lengthways and cut into roughly 1cm slices
- 400g can chopped tomatoes
- 400g can chickpeas, drained and rinsed
- 200g frozen spinach
- 1 tsp soft light brown sugar
- 400ml hot vegetable stock (made with 1 stock cube)
- cooked basmati rice, plain or soya yoghurt and assorted chutneys and pickles

Prep Time: less than 30 mins
Cooking Time: 4 hours
Servings: 4

Ingredients

For the hotpot
- 2 tbsp sunflower oil
- 1 small butternut squash (approximately 800g), scrubbed, deseeded and chopped into chunks
- 2 onions, thinly sliced
- 3 carrots, peeled and cut into chunks
- 2 parsnips, peeled and cut into chunks
- 2 tbsp plain flour
- 400g tin chopped tomatoes
- 2 tbsp tomato purée
- ½ tsp dried chilli flakes (optional)
- 3 tbsp pesto (optional)
- 350ml hot vegetable stock (made with 1 stock cube)
- 100g young spinach leaves (optional)
- salt and freshly ground black pepper

For the dumplings
- 200g self-raising flour
- 75g frozen butter (or 75g shredded vegetarian suet)
- 125ml cold water
- salt and freshly ground black pepper

Vegetarian hotpot with Dumplings

Directions
1. Heat the oil in a large non-stick skillet over medium-high heat. Add the vegetables, in batches if necessary, and cook, stirring regularly, until lightly browned, 4 to 5 minutes. Season with salt and pepper.
2. Place the vegetables in the slow cooker, sprinkle over the flour and stir well. Add chopped tomatoes, tomato puree, chilli flakes and pesto if using and stir again.
3. Pour over the broth and stir. Cover with the lid and cook using the high setting for 4 hours.
4. After 3½ hours, it's time to prepare the dumplings. Place the flour in a large bowl and season with salt and pepper.
5. Coarsely grate a quarter of the butter into the flour.
6. Stir the mixture to lightly coat the butter with the flour. Add the remaining butter in three more batches, grating and stirring in the same way. This should prevent the dumpling dough from clumping together and creating light, fluffy dumplings.
7. Add enough cold water to combine the mixture into a light, fluffy dough. Divide into 12 (or more) equal pieces and roll each into a ball.
8. Stir in the slow cooker the spinach until wilted, then carefully place the dumplings on top. Cover again with the lid and cook on the high setting for an additional 25 to 30 minutes, or until the dumplings are puffy and fluffy.
9. Spoon the hotpot onto serving platters with the dumplings on top

Nutritions: Calories 513; Fat 23 g; Protein 10 g; Carbs 71 g; Fibre 12 g; Sugar 11 g

Onion soup

Prep Time: less than 30 mins
Cooking Time: 6-8 hours
Servings: 4

Ingredients
- 30g butter, diced
- 800g onions, thinly sliced
- 1½ tsp roughly chopped thyme leaves (optional)
- 1½ tsp sugar
- 1.2 litres beef or vegetable stock (made from 2 beef or vegetable stock cubes)

Directions
1. Toss the butter, onions, thyme (if using) and sugar together in the bowl of the slow cooker. Put the lid on and cook using the high setting for 6–8 hours, stirring every so often, until the onions are rich and caramelised.
2. Pour in the stock and cook for another 30 minutes. Serve hot.

Nutritions: Calories 166; Fat 6 g; Protein 6 g; Carbs 21 g; Fibre 3 g; Sugar 9 g

Aubergine, Olive & Raisin Tagine

Prep Time: 10 minutes
Cooking Time: 2 hours 40 minutes
Servings: 5

Directions

1. Finely mince the garlic and dice the onions. Slice the aubergines lengthwise and then halve into thin strips. Rub salt into the aubergines to draw out any bitter moisture. Drain the water or oil out of the jar of olives.
2. In a bowl, combine the cumin, paprika, chilli powder, vinegar, cayenne pepper, turmeric, garlic, and three-quarters of the olive oil (3 tablespoons).
3. Heat a large skillet with the remaining olive oil (1 tablespoon) over medium heat and cook the onions for about 6-7 minutes.
4. Add the spice blend to the pan and cook for 1 more minute until the garlic is nicely fragrant.
5. Pour the vegetable broth into the slow cooker. Add the sliced aubergines, raisins, seasoned onions, and olives to the slow cooker. Season with salt, pepper, and coriander. Stir well to fully combine.
6. Cover and cook on low for 2.5 hours, making sure to stir twice over the course of that time.
7. Serve alone or with couscous.

Ingredients

- 700ml vegetable broth
- 400g pitted green olives (1 jar)
- 60g raisins
- 5 garlic cloves
- 2 aubergines
- 2 white onions
- 4 tbsps olive oil
- 2 tbsps cumin
- 2 tbsps paprika
- 1 tbsp coriander
- 1 tbsp chilli powder
- 1 tsp red wine vinegar
- 1 tsp cayenne pepper
- 1 tsp turmeric

Nutritions: Calories 312; Fat 19 g; Protein 7.5 g; Carbs 34 g; Fibre 12g

Chapter 5
MAIN DISH RECIPES

Macaroni Cheese in Slow Cooker

Prep Time: 5 minutes
Cooking Time: 1 ½ hours
Servings: 6

Directions
1. In a slow cooker, place the macaroni along with mozzarella and cheddar. Pour the condensed milk over the macaroni and add 700 ml of water. Season with pepper and stir.
2. Cover and cook using the High setting for 1 1/2 hour, or until all cheese is melted and pasta is almost tender.
3. Stir well, then cover and cook for a further 15 minutes, or until the macaroni are tender but holding their shape.
4. Serve immediately.

Nutritions: Calories 402; Fat 20 g; Protein 21 g; Carbs 29 g; Fibre 0 g; Sugar 3 g

Ingredients
- 400g dried macaroni
- 200g extra mature cheddar, coarsely grated
- 200g ready-grated mozzarella, from a packet
- 410g can evaporated milk
- freshly ground black pepper

Prep Time: less than 30 minutes
Cooking Time: 5-6 hours
Servings: 4

Ingredients

- 2 tsp vegetable oil, plus 2-3 tbsp for frying the aubergine
- 400g lamb mince
- 1 onion, finely chopped
- 3 garlic cloves, crushed
- 1 tbsp dried oregano
- 1 tsp ground cinnamon
- 2 fresh or dried bay leaves (optional)
- 1 jar passata (690g)
- 1 tsp sugar
- 1 large, or 2 small aubergines, cut into 1½–2cm cubes
- 350g small or baby new potatoes
- salt and freshly ground black pepper
- For the topping
- 40g butter
- 40g plain flour
- 400ml milk
- 50g Parmesan (or extra mature cheddar), finely grated
- 1 free-range egg

Moussaka in the Slow Cooker

Directions

1. Heat up the slow cooker by turning it to the High setting.
2. Heat 2 teaspoons vegetable oil in a pan and brown the lamb, breaking it up with a wooden spoon. If you like, you can drain excess fat. Reduce the slow cooker to the Low setting then place the ground beef in it.
3. Add onion, garlic, oregano, cinnamon, bay leaves if using, passata and 250ml water. Season with a little salt and pepper and add the sugar. Cook on low for 2½ to 3 hours.
4. Meanwhile, clean the lamb pan and heat 1 tablespoon of vegetable oil in it. Cook the aubergine cubes in two batches, using the remaining oil for the second batch, over high heat until golden brown then set aside.
5. Stir the aubergine and potatoes into the slow cooker mixture and cook using the low setting for an additional 3 hours, until potatoes are tender. Stir halfway through cooking.
6. Meanwhile, for the topping, melt the butter and flour in a saucepan for 2 minutes. Gradually add the milk and keep stirring over medium-high heat, until the sauce starts to bubble.
7. Remove from heat and add grated cheese. Season with salt and pepper, set aside for 2 minutes, then beat in the egg.
8. Place the lamb mixture in a shallow casserole dish and preheat the grill.
9. Season the lamb with the salt and pepper and, if the sauce has thickened too much, add 100ml water to loosen it. Pour the béchamel sauce over it and grill until it becomes golden brown.

Tips

This is an ideal dish to prepare ahead of time. Simply assemble in the casserole dish and refrigerate for up to 24 hours or freeze for up to 2 months. In this case instead of grilling, you can bake in a preheated oven at 200°C fan/gas mark 6 for about 30 to 35 minutes, until the lamb sauce is bubbling around the edges and the top is browned.

Nutritions: Calories 700; Fat 46 g; Protein 27 g; Carbs 43 g; Fibre 8 g; Sugar 16 g

Minestrone with Lardons

Prep Time: 15 minutes
Cooking Time: 4 hours
Servings: 4

Ingredients
- 100g smoked, dry-cured lardons
- 2 carrots, roughly chopped
- 2 sticks celery, sliced
- 1 onion, roughly chopped
- 2 garlic cloves, crushed
- 2 sprigs fresh rosemary, needles finely chopped
- 1 tsp dried thyme
- 1 tbsp tomato purée
- 400g can chopped plum tomatoes
- 1.2 litres good-quality chicken stock
- 400g can cannellini beans in water, rinsed and drained
- 50g spaghetti, snapped into short lengths
- 100g head baby leaf or spring greens, thickly shredded
- Salt and freshly ground black pepper
- 2 tbsp extra virgin olive oil
- 25g parmesan, grated (optional)

Directions
1. Place a frying pan over low heat, add the lardons and cook them until the meat results crispy and golden brown and the fat has drained, about 10 minutes. Transfer to a plate.
2. At this point we will use the bacon fat to sauté the carrots, celery, and onion. Cook for two minutes then add the garlic, herbs, and tomato puree. Cook for another minute and finally add the tomatoes and most of the broth. Bring the mixture to a boil.
3. Carefully transfer soup to slow cooker, cover, then cook using the High setting for 4 hours until vegetables are tender.
4. Stir beans and pasta into soup; if the suop seems too thick add the rest of the stock. Scatter the chopped veggies over the soup, then cover with the lid again. Cook for 30 minutes until the pasta is soft.
5. Adjust with salt and pepper, then serve in bowls with a little oil and plenty of parmesan.

Nutritions: Calories 287; Fat 15 g; Protein 15 g; Carbs 23 g; Fibre 3 g; Sugar 8 g

Easy Spaghetti Bolognese

Prep Time: 10 minutes
Cooking Time: 4-8 hours
Servings: 4

Directions

1. In a large nonstick pan, add the ground beef and onion and sear over medium-high heat, about 4 minutes, stirring and pressing against the sides of the pan with a couple of wooden spoons to break up the ground beef as much as possible.
2. Add the garlic and fry for another 1 minute. Place the ground beef and onions in the slow cooker and add the mushrooms, tomatoes, broth, tomato puree and herbs.
3. Season with salt and black pepper.
4. Cover with the lid and cook using the High setting for 4-5 hours or on low for 6-8 hours.
5. When done, serve the bolognese sauce with freshly cooked spaghetti, some grated cheese and basil to taste.

Nutritions: Calories 309; Fat 16 g; Protein 27 g; Carbs 11 g; Fibre 3 g; Sugar 5 g

Ingredients

- 500g beef mince
- 1 medium onion, finely chopped
- 2 garlic cloves, crushed
- 200g mushrooms, any kind, sliced
- 400g tin chopped tomatoes
- 275ml hot beef stock, made with 1 beef stock cube
- 4 tbsp tomato purée
- 2 tsp dried oregano
- 2 dried bay leaves, or 1 fresh
- salt and black pepper
- freshly cooked spaghetti, grated cheese and basil, to serve

Prep Time: 15 minutes
Cooking Time: 2-3 hours
Servings: 4

Ingredients

- 25g butter, diced
- 1 onion, finely chopped
- 1 large garlic cloves, sliced
- 1 large fennel bulb, trimmed and diced, green leaves reserved for garnish
- 1.5 litres hot vegetable stock
- 350g arborio rice
- 50g of grated Parmesan, plus extra to serve (optional)
- 3 tbsp double cream
- 2 unwaxed lemons, zest of 2 and juice of 1
- 80g rocket leaves
- 10g basil leaves
- salt

Risotto with Fennel, Lemon and Rocket

Directions

1. Preheat the slow cooker turning it to the highest setting. Add the butter, onion, garlic and fennel to it. Pour in 1.1 litre of hot stock and cook for 2 hours, or until the fennel and onion are very tender.
2. Using a slotted spoon, transfer about half the vegetables from the slow cooker to a food processor or blender. Mix and add just enough broth to make a really smooth, silky puree.
3. Pour the puree in the slow cooker and add the risotto rice. Cover with the lid and cook until rice is tender and creamy. Start checking after 45 minutes, and if the risotto is not ready, check every 5 minutes thereafter. It should be cooked through in an hour.
4. Once cooked, turn off the slow cooker and stir the parmesan and cream into the risotto. Add most of the lemon zest and juice. If too thick, loosen with up to 200ml of the extra stock. If you need extra liquid, use boiling water.
5. In a food processor or blender, place half the rocket leaves with the last 100ml of the stock, the basil leaves and a good pinch of salt.
6. Blend to a purée, scraping the sides a few times.
7. Swirl the rocket puree through the risotto and serve in bowls.
8. You can top the risotto with rocket leaves, lemon zest and fennel fronds and, if desired, additional grated Parmesan cheese.

Nutritions: Calories 434; Fat 9 g; Protein 9 g; Carbs 73 g; Fibre 1 g; Sugar 1 g

Prep Time: 25 minutes
Cooking Time: 5-8 hours
Servings: 6

Ingredients

- 500g lamb mince
- 1 medium onion, finely chopped
- 1 celery stick, trimmed and thinly sliced (optional)
- 2 tbsp plain flour
- 275ml hot lamb stock, made with 1 stock cube
- 3 tbsp tomato purée
- 3 tbsp Worcestershire sauce
- 3–4 medium carrots, about 300g, peeled and cut into 1.5cm chunks
- 1 tsp dried mixed herbs
- salt and freshly ground black pepper

For the potato topping

- 1.2kg potatoes, ideally Maris Piper, peeled and cut into 3–4cm chunks
- 75g butter, cubed
- 100ml milk

Shepherd's Pie in Slow Cooker

Directions

1. In a large nonstick pan, add the ground beef, onion, and celery and sear over medium-high heat, about 5 minutes, stirring and squishing with a couple of wooden spoons the meat to the sides of the pan to break the mince
2. Transfer the content of the pan to the slow cooker and mix with flour. Mix the hot broth with the tomato puree and Worcestershire sauce and pour over the ground beef. Add carrots and herbs. Season with salt and black pepper and stir well.
3. Cover with the lid and cook using the High setting for 4 to 5½ hours or on low for 7 to 9 hours. (Cook an additional 10 minutes if not going to bake later.)
4. Preheat the oven to 220ºC/200CFan/Gas 7.
5. Twenty minutes before the ground beef is done, simmer the potatoes in a large saucepan of water for about 15 minutes or until tender. Drain well, then return to the pan and add the butter along with plenty of salt and pepper.
6. Mash together. Add the milk and mix everything until smooth. (Heat the milk first if you're not going to bake it in the oven later.)
7. Place the ground beef mixture in a shallow casserole dish and use a large tablespoon to spread the mashed potatoes over it. Start on the outside of the casserolle and work towards the middle.
8. Bake for 25-30 minutes or until lightly golden on top.
9. Serve with the vegetables of your choice

Nutritions: Calories 504; Fat 29 g; Protein 18 g; Carbs 39 g; Fibre 5 g; Sugar 5 g

Sausage Casserole with Vegetables

Prep Time: 10 minutes
Cooking Time: 5-9 hours
Servings: 4

Ingredients
- 2 tbsp vegetable or sunflower oil
- 1 medium onion, thinly sliced
- 12 chipolata sausages
- 3–4 medium carrots, around 300g, peeled and cut into 2cm slices
- 600g medium floury potatoes, preferably Maris Piper, peeled and cut into 3–4cm chunks
- 400g tin chopped tomatoes
- 200ml hot chicken or vegetable stock, made with 1 stock cube
- 3 tbsp tomato purée
- 1 tsp dried mixed herbs
- salt and freshly ground black pepper

1. Heat 1 tablespoon oil in a large non-stick pan and sauté onion over high heat until lightly browned, stirring frequently, 3-4 minutes. Once ready add to the slow cooker.
2. Add remaining oil to the pan and fry sausages over medium-high heat for 4-5 minutes, or until browned on all sides.
3. While cooking the sausages, add the chopped carrots, potatoes and tomatoes to the slow cooker.
4. Mix the hot broth with the tomato puree and the herbs. Pour into the slow cooker and season with salt and pepper; mix well.
5. Place the sausages on top of the tomato and vegetable mixture, without stirring, to help them retain their colour and texture.
6. Cover with the lid and cook using the High setting for 5 to 6 hours or with the low one for 7 to 9 hours.

Nutritions: Calories 677; Fat 45 g; Protein 23 g; Carbs 41 g; Fibre 6 g; Sugar 9 g

Beef Casserole

Prep Time: 30 minutes
Cooking Time: 8-10 hours
Servings: 4

Directions
1. In a large bowl, place the meat with the red wine, the peeled garlic cloves, the sliced onions, the orange peel and the bay leaf. Season with salt and pepper and mix everything together. Cover the bowl with cling film and refrigerate for 30 minutes or overnight if you are going to cook in the morning.
2. Add the olive oil to and bacon lardons to the bottom of the slow cooker.
3. Pour half of the meat and its marinade into the slow cooker. Add the carrots, then top with the remaining meat.
4. Cover the slow cooker and cook using the High setting for 8-10 hours.
5. When ready, add the chopped parsley and black olives. Serve the casserole with creamy mash or rice.

Nutritions: Calories 448; Fat 30 g; Protein 24 g; Carbs 10 g; Fibre 2 g; Sugar 3 g

Ingredients
- 500g braising steak, brisket or shin of beef cut into 2cm/1in chunks
- 150ml red wine
- 3 garlic cloves
- 2 medium onions, sliced
- 1 strip orange peel
- 1 bay leaf
- 1 tsp olive oil
- 100g smoked bacon lardons
- 2 carrots, sliced
- 1 tbsp chopped parsley
- handful black olives
- salt and freshly ground black pepper

Chapter 6
DESSERTS

Clotted Cream Fudge

Prep Time: 15 minutes
Cooking Time: 5 hours
Makes: 16 squares

Directions
1. In the slow cooker, combine the caster sugar, golden syrup, clotted cream, vanilla, and a pinch of salt. Stir until well combined and smooth.
2. Cook using the High setting for 4 to 5 hours, stirring every 30 minutes, or until it reaches a golden caramel and glossy look. If your slow cooker works without a lid, cook uncovered to speed up cooking. It takes about 5 hours if you're using a multi-function cooker with a locked lid that requires constant opening and stirring.
3. Grease a 20 cm baking tin and line with baking paper. Carefully remove the bowl from the slow cooker and set it on a heat-safe surface or cutting board. Mix vigorously with a wooden spoon or spatula for 10-15 minutes to cool the fudge and break up large sugar crystals.
4. The fudge will thicken as it cools and will begin to look matte. Tip into the tin and smooth the surface using a spatula.
5. Sprinkle with a little more salt and chill until set, about 1 hour.
6. Cut into pieces. It will keep for five days in an airtight container.

Ingredients
- 300g golden caster sugar
- 100g golden syrup
- 200g clotted cream
- 2 tsp vanilla extract
- vegetable oil, for the tin

Nutritions: Calories 126; Fat 3 g; Protein 1 g; Carbs 24 g; Fibre 0 g; Sugar 21 g

Hot Chocolate in Slow Cooker

Prep Time: 5 minutes
Cooking Time: 2 hours
Servings: 8 – 10

Ingredients
- 1l milk
- 300ml double cream
- 200g dark chocolate, chopped
- 100g milk chocolate, chopped
- scorched marshmallows, to serve
- softly whipped cream, to serve
- grated chocolate, to serve

Directions
1. Pour the milk and cream into the slow cooker. Add the dark and milk chocolate, cover and cook on the Low setting for 2 hours, stirring halfway through cooking.
2. Remove the lid and stir again, then cook for a further 15-20 minutes. Serve in mugs and garnish with marshmallows, dollops of cream and grated chocolate.

Nutritions: Calories 261; Fat 17 g; Protein 4 g; Carbs 20 g; Fibre 2 g; Sugar 15 g

Hot Chocolate Fondant Cake

Prep Time: 15 minutes
Cooking Time: 3-5 hours
Servings: 8

Directions
1. Butter the bottom and sides of the slow cooker bowl. In a stand mixer fitted with the whisk attachment or with an electric mixer, cream together the butter and both sugars. Add the eggs one at a time, then flour, cocoa, baking powder, espresso, pinch of salt and chocolate.
2. Add just the right amount of milk to help the batter pull away from the spatula in big dollops. Pour into prepared slow cooker.
3. In a heatproof bowl, combine the sauce ingredients with 300ml boiling water, then carefully pour over the batter in the slow cooker.
4. Cover with the lid and cook using the Low setting for 5-6 hours or on high for 3 hours, until cake springs back when pressed and has risen well.
5. Serve with crème fraîche, whipped cream or vanilla ice cream.

Nutritions: Calories 350; Fat 17 g; Protein 7 g; Carbs 41 g; Fibre 4 g; Sugar 17 g

Ingredients
- 100g of butter, plus extra for greasing the slow cooker
- 90g golden caster sugar
- 50g of light brown soft sugar
- 3 eggs
- 250g self-raising flour
- 50g cocoa powder
- 1 tsp baking powder
- 1/2 tsp instant espresso powder
- 100g dark chocolate, chopped (or use dark
- chocolate chips)
- 100-150ml milk
- crème fraîche, whipped cream or vanilla ice
- cream, to serve

For the sauce
- 200g light brown soft sugar
- 25g cocoa powder
- 1/2 tsp instant espresso powder
- 1/2 tsp vanilla extract

Prep Time: 20 minutes
Cooking Time: 2 hours
Servings: 8

Ingredients

- 1 tbsp butter to grease
- 8 sponge fingers (boudoir biscuits)
- 500g full fat cream cheese
- 80g caster sugar
- 3 eggs
- 100ml double cream
- 2 tsp vanilla extract
- 1 tsp lemon zest finely grated
- 2 tbsp lemon juice

For the topping

- 3 clementines or satsumas peeled and sliced
- 2-3 tbsp pomegranate seeds
- 1 little icing sugar for sprinkling
- a few mint leaves

Clementine & Pomegranate Cheesecake

Directions

1. Preheat the slow cooker if necessary (check the instructions of your slow cooker).
2. Grease a 15 cm diameter straight-sided baking dish or soufflé dish with butter, then coat the bottom and sides with baking parchment. It's best not to use a tin, as the slow cooker cooks the cheesecake in a bain-marie style and you want to avoid any seepage. Arrange the sponge fingers over the base of the dish, trimming them to fit.
3. In a large bowl, beat cream cheese until soft, then add powdered sugar and beat again until smooth.
4. In a separate bowl, whisk together the eggs, cream, and vanilla paste or extract. Gradually add this to the cream cheese mixture, then add the lemon zest and lemon juice. Place in the previously prepared dish and cover tightly with a piece of buttered aluminium foil.
5. Place in the slow cooker and add enough boiled water to reach about halfway up the sides of the dish. Cover with the lid and cook using the High setting until set, 2-2½ hours.
6. Using oven gloves, carefully remove from the slow cooker. Let the cheesecake cool completely (it will shrink a bit). Once chilled, refrigerate for several hours or overnight.
7. To serve, run a knife around the edge of the dish and turn out the cake onto a board or plate.
8. Remove the parchment paper. Place a serving platter on top, then carefully turn over so the cheesecake is facing up.
9. To decorate, place clementine slices or satsumas on top of the cheesecake and sprinkle with pomegranate seeds. Dust with some icing sugar and add a few mint leaves if you like.

Nutritions: Calories 315; Fat 26 g; Protein 6 g; Carbs 14 g; Fibre 0 g; Sugar 12 g

Prep Time: 15 minutes
Cooking Time: 3 hours
Servings: 4

Ingredients
- 125g of butter (plus extra for greasing)
- 125g light muscovado or light soft brown sugar
- 2 eggs
- The zest of 1 orange
- 1 tsp of orange extract or vanilla extract
- 2 tbsp fine-shred orange marmalade
- 110g of self-raising flour
- pinch of salt
- 1/4 tsp baking powder
- 15g of cocoa powder
- 2 tbsp milk
- A pack of Galaxy Minstrels (40 g)
- crème fraiche or whipped cream and fine shreds of orange zest to serve

Equipment
- 1-litre pudding basin

Chocolate Orange Sponge Pudding

Directions
1. Refer to the instructions for your slow cooker and preheat if necessary. Grease a 1.2 liters pudding basin with a little butter.
2. In a large bowl, cream the butter and sugar until light and fluffy. Gradually add the eggs, then add the orange zest, orange extract or vanilla extract and jam.
3. Sieve the flour, salt, baking powder, and cocoa powder, then gently mix them into the creamy mixture using a large spoon. Add milk and the minstrels. Transfer the mixture to the basin and level the surface. Cover tightly with a lid or a piece of buttered foil.
4. Lift the pudding bowl into the slow cooker and add enough boiled water to come roughly halfway up the sides
5. Cover the slow cooker and cook using the High setting for 3-3½ hours.
6. Using oven gloves, carefully lift the basin out of the slow cooker. Remove the lid or foil, then run a knife around the rim of the basin and invert it onto a serving platter.
7. Divide into bowls and serve with dollops of crème fraiche or whipped cream and a few strips of orange zest.

Tip: You can use a packet of chocolate buttons instead of Minstrels.

Nutritions: Calories 395; Fat 23 g; Protein 6 g; Carbs 42 g; Fibre 2 g; Sugar 24 g

Apple Crumble in Slow Cooker

Prep Time: 14 minutes
Cooking Time: 3 hours 30 mins
Servings: 4

Ingredients
- 5 apples, peeled, cored and each cut into 8 wedges
- 1 tsp ground cinnamon
- 1 orange, zested and half juiced
- 55g rolled oats
- 50g walnut pieces
- ½ tsp ground ginger
- 70g plain flour
- 80g light muscovado sugar
- 85g unsalted butter, melted

Directions
1. Place the apple slices in the slow cooker. Sprinkle over them the ground cinnamon, orange zest, 1 tablespoon juice and then mix together.
2. In a food processor, combine the rolled oats and walnuts and pulse a few times to create a breadcrumb texture. Pour into a bowl.
3. Stir the flour, ginger, and sugar into the mixture, then add the butter and mix well.
4. Pour the crumble mixture over the apples, covering them all. Cover the crumble with two sheets of kitchen paper or kitchen roll. Cover the slow cooker with the lid and cook using the Low setting for 3½ hours.
5. Remove the kitchen paper and cook with the lid slightly ajar for the last 10 minutes.

Nutritions: Calories 519; Fat 29 g; Protein 5.9 g; Carbs 63.9 g; Fibre 6.3 g; Sugar 37 g

Boozy Mincemeat Sponge Pudding

Prep Time: 15 minutes
Cooking Time: 3 hours
Servings: 6

Directions

1. Preheat the slow cooker if necessary (Check your slow cooker instructions). Grease a 1.2 liters pudding basin with butter.
2. Pour the golden syrup into the bottom of the pudding basin. Mix the mincemeat and brandy or rum, then pour half of this mixture over the syrup.
3. In a large bowl, cream together the butter and sugar until light and fluffy. Gradually add the eggs, then the orange zest, lemon zest, and the remaining mincemeat and alcohol mixture.
4. Sieve the flour and salt, then gently fold them into the mixture with the help of a large metal spoon. Add the milk and mix well. Pour into the basin and level the surface.
5. Cover tightly with a lid or a piece of buttered aluminium foil.
6. Lift the pudding bowl into the slow cooker and add enough boiled water to fill it about halfway (the water should come roughly halfway up the sides of the bowl). Cover with the lid and cook using the High setting for 3-3½ hours.
7. Using oven gloves, carefully lift the pudding basin out of the slow cooker. Remove the lid or foil, then run a knife around the edge of the basin and turn out the pudding onto a dish.
8. Spread into bowls and serve with single cream, whipped cream, or brandy butter.

Ingredients

- 125 of butter (plus extra to grease)
- 2 tbsp of golden syrup
- 5 tbsp of mincemeat
- 2 tbsp of brandy or rum
- 125g of caster sugar
- 2 large eggs
- zest of 1 orange
- zest of 1 lemon
- 125g of self-raising flour
- pinch of salt
- 1 tbsp of milk
- single cream, whipped double cream or brandy butter to serve

Nutritions: Calories 280; Fat 15 g; Protein 4 g; Carbs 32 g; Fibre 1 g; Sugar 20 g

Blueberry Cobbler

Prep Time: 5 minutes
Cooking Time: 4 hours
Servings: 6

Ingredients
- 600g blueberries
- 250ml whole milk
- 180g all-purpose flour
- 150g granulated sugar
- 60g butter (softened)
- 2 tbsps cornstarch
- 3 tsps baking powder
- 2 tsps ground cinnamon
- 1 tsp vanilla extract

Directions
1. In a bowl, sift together the flour and baking powder. Add two-thirds of the sugar, softened butter, and a pinch of salt.
2. Stir in the milk and mix slowly to prevent clumps from forming.
3. In a separate bowl, combine the remaining one-third of sugar, vanilla extract, ground cinnamon, and blueberries. Mix together so all the blueberries are coated.
4. Add the batter to the greased slow cooker in an even layer. Top with the sugar-coated blueberries.
5. Cook on low for 4 hours.
6. Serve alone or with vanilla ice cream.

Nutritions: Calories 374; Fat 10 g; Protein 5 g; Carbs 69 g; Fibre 4 g

RECIPES INDEX

A
Aloo gobi in Slow Cooker 47
Apple Crumble in Slow Cooker 76
Aubergine, Olive & Raisin Tagine 55

B
Banana Bread for Breakfast 17
Barbecue-style Pork Chops 31
Beef Brisket with Bean Mash 35
Beef Casserole 67
Beef Hotpot 30
Beef Stew Easy Recipe 23
Blueberry Cobbler 78
Boozy Mincemeat
Sponge Pudding 77
Butter Chicken 44
Butternut Squash Mac & Cheese 50

C
Chicken Cacciatore in Slow Cooker 39
Chicken Korma 37
Chicken shawarma in Slow Cooker .. 41
Chicken Tacos 43
Chinese-style Beef 28

Chocolate Orange
Sponge Pudding 75
Clementine & Pomegranate
Cheesecake 73
Clotted Cream Fudge 69

D
Dhal in Slow Cooker 49

E
Easy chilli 22
Easy Pulled Pork 20
Easy Spaghetti Bolognese 61
Egg and Broccoli Casserole 14

G
Goulash in Slow Cooker 33

H
Harissa Vegetable Stew 46
Hominy for Breakfast 16
Honey Mustard Chicken 42
Hot Chocolate Fondant Cake 71
Hot Chocolate in Slow Cooker 70

L
Lamb Osso Bucco 21
Lamb Rogan Josh 29

M
Macaroni Cheese in Slow Cooker 57
Massaman Curry 25
Minestrone with Lardons 60
Moussaka in the Slow Cooker 59

O
Onion soup 54

P
Pork shoulder with butterbeans,
apple, and sage 24

R
Rice pudding with Jam 13

Risotto with Fennel,
Lemon and Rocket 63
Roast beef in Slow Cooker 27

S
Sausage and Lentil Casserole 34
Sausage Casserole
with Vegetables 66
Shepherd's Pie in Slow Cooker 65
Smoky Breakfast Casserole 15
Spring Chicken and Herb Soup 38

V
Vegetarian hotpot with Dumplings .. 53
Veggie Slow Cooker Curry 51
Veggie-Style Bolognese 48

W
Welsh Rarebit 18

Printed in Great Britain
by Amazon